Collins

Grammar, Punctuation and Vocabulary Progress Tests

Year 3/P4

Author:
Abigail Steel

Series editor:
Stephanie Austwick

William Collins' dream of knowledge for all began with the publication of his first book in 1819. A self-educated mill worker, he not only enriched millions of lives, but also founded a flourishing publishing house. Today, staying true to this spirit, Collins books are packed with inspiration, innovation and practical expertise. They place you at the centre of a world of possibility and give you exactly what you need to explore it.

Collins. Freedom to teach.

Published by Collins
An imprint of HarperCollins*Publishers*
The News Building
1 London Bridge Street
London SE1 9GF

Browse the complete Collins catalogue at www.collins.co.uk

© HarperCollins*Publishers* Limited 2019

10 9 8 7 6 5 4 3 2 1

ISBN 978-0-00-833363-8

All rights reserved. No part of this publication may be reproduced, stored in a retrieval system, or transmitted in any form by any means, electronic, mechanical, photocopying, recording or otherwise, without the prior written permission of the Publisher or a licence permitting restricted copying in the United Kingdom issued by the Copyright Licensing Agency Ltd., Barnard's Inn, 86 Fetter Lane, London, EC4A 1EN.

British Library Cataloguing in Publication Data. A catalogue record for this publication is available from the British Library.

Author: Abigail Steel

Series Editor: Stephanie Austwick

Publisher: Katie Sergeant

Product Manager: Sarah Thomas

Content Editor: Holly Woolnough

Copyeditor and proofreader: Tanya Solomons

Reviewer: Rachel Clarke

Internal design and typesetting: Hugh Hillyard-Parker

Cover designers: The Big Mountain Design and Ken Vail Graphic Design

Production Controller: Katharine Willard

Contents

How to use this book 4

Year 3 Curriculum map: Yearly overview 6

Year 3/P4 Half Termly Tests

Autumn Half Term 1 7
Autumn Half Term 2 16
Spring Half Term 1 25
Spring Half Term 2 34
Summer Half Term 1 44
Summer Half Term 2 53

Mark schemes

Autumn Half Term 1 63
Autumn Half Term 2 65
Spring Half Term 1 67
Spring Half Term 2 69
Summer Half Term 1 71
Summer Half Term 2 73

Record sheet 75

How to use this book

Introduction

Collins *Grammar, Punctuation and Vocabulary Progress Tests* have been designed to give you a consistent whole-school approach to teaching and assessing grammar, punctuation and vocabulary. Each photocopiable book covers the required vocabulary, grammar and punctuation objectives from the English National Curriculum statutory guidance and vocabulary, grammar and punctuation appendix. For teachers in Scotland, the books can offer guidance and structure that is not provided in the Curriculum for Excellence Experiences and Outcomes or Benchmarks.

Revision of previous years' work is also included, where appropriate, to ensure children are building their skills to become confident and secure users of grammar, punctuation and vocabulary. As standalone tests, independent of any teaching and learning scheme, the Collins *Grammar, Punctuation and Vocabulary Progress Tests* provide a structured way to assess progress in grammar, punctuation and vocabulary, to help you identify areas for development, and to provide evidence towards expectations for each year group.

Building confidence and understanding

At the end of Key Stage 1 and Key Stage 2, children are assessed on their understanding of grammar, punctuation and vocabulary. This is done through teacher assessment of children's writing, through the grammar, punctuation and vocabulary SAT in KS2 and through the optional SAT in KS1. Collins *Grammar, Punctuation and Vocabulary Progress Tests* have been designed to help children recognise grammatical features whilst building familiarity with the format, language and style of the SATs. Through regular use of the Collins *Grammar, Punctuation and Vocabulary Progress Tests* children should develop and practise the necessary skills to complete the national tests confidently and proficiently.

The Collins *Grammar, Punctuation and Vocabulary Progress Tests* are written so that new grammatical content is presented in a variety of ways with increasing challenge over the tests in the book. Previous learning is also addressed in Years 2 – 6 with questions that ask children to recall grammar, punctuation and vocabulary learned in previous year groups.

How to use this book

In this book, you will find six photocopiable half-termly tests, written to replicate the format of the SATs with space for children to write their answers. You will also find a Curriculum Map on page 6 indicating the aspects of the Content Domain covered in each test and across the year group. These have been cross-referenced with the appropriate age-related statements from the National Curriculum. In KS2, each test should take 35 – 45 minutes to complete and in KS1 each test should take approximately 20 minutes. KS1 teachers may prefer to administer each test in two halves of 10 minutes each, and in Year 1 read each question to children.

To help you mark the tests, you will find mark schemes that include the number of marks to be awarded, model answers and a reference to the elements of the Content Domain covered by each question.

Test demand

The tests have been written to ensure smooth progression in children's understanding of grammar, punctuation and vocabulary within the book and across the rest of the books in the series. Each test builds on those before it so that children are guided towards the expectations of the SATs at the end of KS1 and KS2.

Year 3: How to use this book

Year group	Number of marks per test
1	20
2	20
3	30
4	30
5	40
6	50

Performance thresholds

The table below provides guidance for assessing how children perform in the tests. Most children should achieve scores at or above the expected standard with some children working at greater depth and exceeding expectations for their year group. Whilst these threshold bands do not represent standardised scores, as in the end of key stage SATs, they will give an indication of how children are performing against the expected standard for their year group.

Year group	Working towards	Expected standard	Greater depth
1	9 marks or below	10–16 marks	17–20 marks
2	9 marks or below	10–16 marks	17–20 marks
3	14 marks or below	15–25 marks	26–30 marks
4	14 marks or below	15–25 marks	26–30 marks
5	18 marks or below	19–33 marks	34–40 marks
6	23 marks or below	24–42 marks	43–50 marks

Tracking progress

A record sheet is provided to help you illustrate to children the areas in which they have performed well and where they need to develop. A spreadsheet tracker is also provided via **collins.co.uk/assessment/downloads** which enables you to identify whole-class patterns of attainment. This can then be used to inform your next teaching and learning steps.

Editable download

All the files are available in Word and PDF format for you to edit if you wish. Go to **collins.co.uk/assessment/downloads** to find instructions on how to download. The files are password protected and the password clue is included on the website. You will need to use the clue to locate the password in your book. You can use these editable files to help you meet the specific needs of your class, whether that be by increasing or decreasing the challenge, by reducing the number of questions, by providing more space for answers or increasing the size of text as required for specific children.

© HarperCollinsPublishers Ltd 2019

Year 3 Curriculum map: Yearly overview

National Curriculum objective (Year 3)	Content domain	Autumn Test 1	Autumn Test 2	Spring Test 1	Spring Test 2	Summer Test 1	Summer Test 2
WORD							
Formation of nouns using a range of prefixes [for example, *super-; anti-, auto-*]	G1 G6				●		●
Use of determiners *a* or *an* according to whether the next word begins with a consonant or a vowel [for example, *a rock, an open box*]	G1	●	●	●		●	●
Word families based on common words, showing how words are related in form and meaning [for example, *solve, solution, solver, dissolve, insoluble*]	G6		●	●		●	●
SENTENCE							
Expressing time, place and cause using conjunctions [for example, *when, before, after, while, so, because*]	G1	●		●			●
Expressing time, place and cause using adverbs [for example, *then, next, soon, therefore*]	G1		●		●		●
Expressing time, place and cause using prepositions [for example, *before, after, during, in, because of*]	G1					●	●
TEXT							
Use of the present perfect form of verbs instead of the simple past [for example, *He has gone out to play* contrasted with *He went out to play*]	G4		●		●	●	●
PUNCTUATION							
Introduce to inverted commas to punctuate direct speech	G5	●			●		●

Content Domain Key
G1: Grammatical terms / word clauses
G2: Functions of sentences
G3: Combining words, phrases and clauses
G4: Verb forms, tenses and consistency
G5: Punctuation
G6: Vocabulary
G7: Standard English and formality

Autumn Half Term 1

1 Draw a line to match each word to a **suffix** to make **four** different adjectives.
Use each suffix only once.

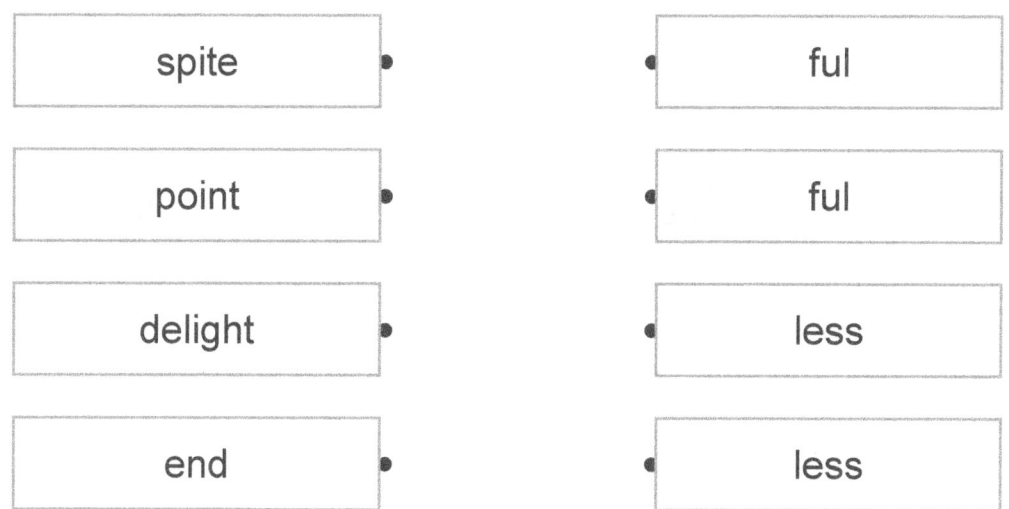

1 mark

2 Insert a **comma** in the correct place in the sentence below.

I have apple melon and grapes in my fruit salad.

1 mark

3 The verbs in the sentence below should be in the **past**. Circle **one** word that needs to be changed.

On Saturday we went swimming and I wear my new swimming goggles.

1 mark

4 Which sentence is a **question**?

Tick **one**.

When Sam comes home I'll tidy up. ☐

Where did you put your bag? ☐

What an exciting match that was! ☐

I'd like to know why Ben was upset. ☐

1 mark

5 Add a **suffix** to the words in the boxes to complete the sentences.

We felt _____ when the rain finally stopped.

cheer

It was going to be a noisy and _____ night.

sleep

1 mark

6 Underline the **noun phrase** in the sentence below.

We travelled on the big red bus.

1 mark

7 Tick the correct option to complete the sentence below.

I _____ like bananas.

Tick **one**.

don't ☐

do'nt ☐

d'ont ☐

dont' ☐

1 mark

8 Tick **one** box in each row to show whether each sentence should end with a **full stop** or a **question mark**.

Sentence	Full stop	Question mark
When can we go to the library		
When the music plays, I will sing		
When will the film start		

2 marks

9 Write the words <u>has not</u> as one word, using an **apostrophe**.

The new café in town <u>has not</u> opened yet.

☐

1 mark

10 Tick **one** box in each row to show whether the sentence is an **exclamation** or a **statement**.

Sentence	Exclamation	Statement
The leaves are turning yellow		
I think I will need gloves today		
What a cold morning it is		

2 marks

11 Tick the sentence that shows what the cat is doing now.

Tick **one**.

The cat stretched her paws. ☐

The cat slept on the cushion. ☐

The cat is eating her dinner. ☐

The cat walked along the wall. ☐

1 mark

12 Write a **command** a teacher might say in the classroom. Remember to use correct punctuation.

2 marks

13 Add **two commas** to the sentence below to make it clear that Ravi has four things on his desk.

Ravi has a lamp a book his calculator and a pot of pencils on his desk.

1 mark

14 Circle the word that shows the sentence below is in the **present**.

Miss Jones is at the market.

1 mark

15 Which option is punctuated correctly?

Tick **one**.

Ann loves writing stories she writes every day ☐

ann loves writing stories She writes every day. ☐

Ann loves writing stories. She writes every day. ☐

ann loves writing stories. she writes every day ☐

1 mark

16 Circle the two words that need a **capital letter** in the sentence below.

my favourite day of the week is tuesday.

1 mark

17 What is the grammatical term for the underlined part of the sentence?

Seema ran <u>the last race</u> and finished first!

Tick **one**.

fronted adverbial ☐

noun phrase ☐

main clause ☐

exclamation ☐

1 mark

18 Tick **one** box in each row to show whether each sentence is in the **past progressive** or **present progressive**.

Sentence	Past progressive	Present progressive
Kate was tidying up.		
Joshi is listening to music.		
Bill is walking his dog.		

2 marks

19 Insert an **apostrophe** in the correct place in the sentence below.

Those are Peters pencils.

1 mark

20 Tick the correct option to complete the sentence below.

Lennox walked through ____ open door in the library.

Tick **one**.

a ☐
an ☐
some ☐
those ☐

1 mark

21 Which option completes the sentence in the **past progressive**?

The artist _____ his finest work.

Tick **one**.

painted ☐
paints ☐
is painting ☐
was painting ☐

1 mark

22 Tick the correct word to complete the sentence below.

I must take the washing inside _____ it rains.

Tick **one**.

because ☐
so ☐
before ☐
after ☐

1 mark

23 Add **inverted commas** to the sentence below to show what Imran is saying.

Can we go for a bike ride? asked Imran.

1 mark

24 What is the grammatical term for the underlined part of the sentence?

<u>The beautiful green parrot</u> flew through the air.

Tick **one**.

an exclamation ☐

a main clause ☐

a noun phrase ☐

a command ☐

1 mark

25 The verb in the sentence below should be in the **present progressive**. Circle **one** word that needs to be changed.

Grandpa was digging the flowerbeds in his garden.

1 mark

26 Choose the correct word to complete each sentence.
Write the word on the line.

I watched _____ frog hopping into the pond.
　　　　　　↓
　　　　[a / an]

I need _____ envelope for the letter I've written.
　　　　↓
　　[a / an]

We go to the park for _____ hour after school on Fridays.
　　　　　　　　　　　　↓
　　　　　　　　　[a / an]

1 mark

Total: _____ /30

Autumn Half Term 2

1 Write the correct word on the line in the sentence below.

tall   taller   tallest

The children planted seeds. After a few weeks, Samira's seedling was _____ than Evie's.

1 mark

2 Which sentence contains a verb in the **past progressive**?

Tick **one**.

Zack is playing cricket. ☐

Zack was playing cricket. ☐

Zack played cricket. ☐

Zack will play cricket. ☐

1 mark

3 Insert the missing punctuation mark to complete the sentence below.

Can you count to one hundred

1 mark

4 Draw a line to match each **determiner** to the correct sentence.
Use each determiner only once.

Sentence **Determiner**

At the beach I ate ____ ice-cream. — a

I saw _____ big seagull. — the

I thought it was ____ best day ever. — an

1 mark

5 Add **inverted commas** to the sentence below to show what Lara is saying.

I would like pizza for dinner tonight, said Lara.

1 mark

6 Which **word class** is the underlined word in the sentence below?

I saw Philippa today.

Tick **one**.

determiner ☐
adverb ☐
noun ☐
verb ☐

1 mark

7 Add a **suffix** to the word <u>fast</u> to complete the sentence below.

Jamal won the race because he was <u>fast____</u> than the other children.

1 mark

8 Explain why the underlined words start with a **capital letter**.

<u>Lady Grey</u> took a train to <u>Mattock Station</u> on <u>Thursday</u> morning.

_____

_____

1 mark

9 Tick the correct option to complete the sentence below.

Hassan chose to eat ____ apple for his dessert.

Tick **one**.

these ☐

those ☐

a ☐

an ☐

1 mark

10 Which sentence uses **inverted commas** correctly?

Tick **one**.

Would you like to play? "asked Robert." ☐

"Would you like to play"? asked Robert. ☐

"Would you like to play?" asked Robert. ☐

Would you like to "play?" asked Robert. ☐

1 mark

11 Which punctuation mark needs to be added to the sentence below?

What an amazing adventure we had

Tick **one**.

full stop ☐

exclamation mark ☐

question mark ☐

comma ☐

1 mark

12 Write the correct word on the line in the sentence below.

tasty   tastier   tastiest

Mum taught me how to bake cakes, but I think her cakes are still _____ than mine.

1 mark

13 The **verb** in the sentence below should be in the **past progressive**. Circle one word that needs to be changed.

Tammy is watching her favourite show, *Performing Stars*.

1 mark

14 Draw a line to match each **determiner** to the correct sentence.
Use each determiner only once.

Sentence	Determiner
I made _____ model robot.	the
I used _____ old plastic bottle.	an
Then added bits of wood for _____ feet.	a

1 mark

15 Which sentence is an **exclamation**?

Tick **one**.

Did you think of all those ideas? ☐

Ben really enjoys writing. ☐

Can you help Ben finish his story? ☐

What a great story you've written! ☐

1 mark

16 Add a **suffix** to the word cheap to complete the sentence below.

Bananas cost 10p each, which is cheap_____ than apples.

1 mark

17 Tick **one** box in each row to show whether the underlined word in each sentence is an **adverb of time** or an **adverb of place**.

Sentence	Adverb of time	Adverb of place
I will speak to you soon.		
I saw that show yesterday.		
I played the game outdoors.		

2 marks

18 Write a **statement** about how you travel to school. Remember to use correct punctuation.

2 marks

19 Tick **one** box in each row to show whether each sentence is in the **past progressive** or **present progressive**.

Sentence	Past progressive	Present progressive
Emma was playing chess.		
Stan is jumping on the trampoline.		
Pia was brushing her hair.		

2 marks

20 Choose the correct word to complete each sentence. Write the word on the line.

We watched _____ film with my mum at the cinema.

a / an

I drew a picture of _____ ant crawling along a branch.

a / an

I drank _____ big glass of juice when I got home.

a / an

1 mark

21 Write the correct word on the line in the sentence below.

happy   happier   happiest

I like to visit my grandpa. He is always smiling. I think he is the _____ man in the world.

1 mark

22 Which **word class** is the underlined word in the sentence below?

I looked everywhere to find my pen.

Tick **one**.

verb ☐

noun ☐

determiner ☐

adverb ☐

1 mark

23 Add **inverted commas** to the sentence below to show what Oscar is saying.

Oscar shouted, Stop kicking my ball over the fence!

1 mark

24 Which **word class** are the underlined words in the sentence below?

The gymnast did a cartwheel and then an amazing flip.

Tick **one**.

verbs ☐

nouns ☐

determiners ☐

adjectives ☐

1 mark

25 Which **tense** is used in the sentence below?

Dan was climbing a tall tree in his garden.

Tick **one**.

- simple past ☐
- simple present ☐
- past progressive ☐
- present progressive ☐

1 mark

26 Tick **two** boxes to show the correct places for **inverted commas** in the sentence below.

Tick **two**.

Fran said, ↑ What time does the party start? ↑

(ticks before "What" and after "start?")

1 mark

27 Tick the **adverb of place** in the sentence below.

Tick **one**.

It was raining so we went indoors.

1 mark

Total: _____ /30

Year 3: Spring Half Term Test 1

Name: Year: Date:

Spring Half Term 1

1 Circle the **adverb** in the sentence below.

Davinder carefully wrapped the gift for his grandmother.

1 mark

2 The **verb** in the sentence below should be in the **present progressive**. Circle **one** word that needs to be changed.

Harriet was reading an exciting book about

an underwater adventure.

1 mark

3 Which sentence uses **capital letters** correctly?

Tick **one**.

Jed jones, the Pop star, is visiting hull today. ☐

jed Jones, the pop Star, is visiting Hull today. ☐

Jed Jones, the Pop Star, is visiting Hull today. ☐

Jed Jones, the pop star, is visiting Hull today. ☐

1 mark

© HarperCollinsPublishers Ltd 2019

4 Tick **one** box to show where a **comma** should go in the sentence below.

Tick **one**.

Paul bought a bunch of pink yellow and orange flowers.

☐   ☐ ☐   ☐

1 mark

5 Insert an **apostrophe** in the correct place in the sentence below.

That is Isabelles skipping rope.

1 mark

6 Draw a line to match each **prefix** to a word to make **four** different words.
Use each prefix only once.

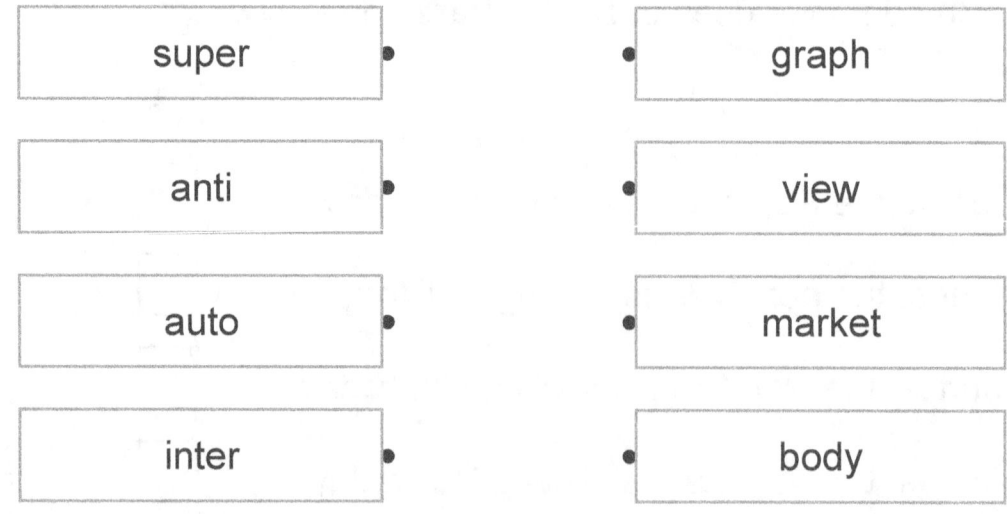

1 mark

7 Write the correct word on the line in the sentence below.

solved   solution   dissolve

Thomas was stuck until Fred gave him the _____ to the problem.

1 mark

8 Tick the correct word to complete the sentence below.

Matt brushed his teeth _____ he went to bed.

Tick **one**.

- yet ☐
- before ☐
- if ☐
- while ☐

1 mark

9 Tick the **adverb** in the sentence below.

Tick **one**.

The children cheered loudly when the music began to play.
⇧   ⇧   ⇧   ⇧

1 mark

10 Insert the missing punctuation mark to complete the sentence below.

What a fast racing car that is

1 mark

11 Which sentence uses a **possessive apostrophe** correctly?

Tick **one**.

Jess went to Todd's party at the weekend. ☐

Jess went to Todds' party at the weekend. ☐

Jes's went to Todds party at the weekend. ☐

Jess' went to Todds party at the weekend. ☐

1 mark

12 Tick **one** box in each row to show whether each sentence is in the **past progressive** or **present progressive**.

Sentence	Past progressive	Present progressive
Maya was riding her bike.		
Eden is playing the trumpet.		
Adam is eating his dinner.		

2 marks

13 What does the root word <u>phone</u> mean in the word family below?

tele**phone**   micro**phone**   **phon**ics   xylo**phone**

Tick **one**.

light ☐

sound ☐

heat ☐

body ☐

1 mark

14 Add two **commas** to the sentence below to make it clear that Tanya has four things in her bag.

Tanya has a purse a hairbrush some gloves and an old shop receipt in her bag.

1 mark

15 Which one **prefix** can be added to all three words below to make new words?
Write the prefix in the box.

_____marine

_____title

_____tract

[   ]

1 mark

16 Which punctuation mark should be used in the space indicated by the arrow?

We found the bus drivers keys.
                              ↑

Tick **one**.

question mark   ☐

exclamation mark   ☐

apostrophe   ☐

comma   ☐

1 mark

17 Complete the sentence below with a word formed from the root word <u>thought</u>.

Everyone said she was a _____ girl.

1 mark

18 Complete the sentence with an appropriate **adverb**.

Eve held the kitten _____.

1 mark

19 Which option completes the sentence in the **present progressive**?

Olivia's mum _____ the lawn.

Tick **one**.

will mow ☐

mowed ☐

is mowing ☐

was mowing ☐

1 mark

20 Which option is punctuated correctly?

Tick **one**.

Janice works in a shop. her shift starts at ten. ☐

Janice works in a shop Her shift starts at ten ☐

janice works in a shop her shift starts at ten. ☐

Janice works in a shop. Her shift starts at ten. ☐

1 mark

21 Draw a line to match each **prefix** to a word to make **four** different words.
Use each prefix only once.

sub	—	formation
re	—	marine
trans	—	take
mis	—	action

1 mark

22 Circle the **conjunction** in the sentence below.

It was raining yet Mrs Hardy refused to use her umbrella.

1 mark

23 Which option uses **commas** correctly?

Tick **one**.

We need, eggs, flour, sugar and, butter. ☐

We need eggs, flour, sugar and butter. ☐

We need eggs, flour sugar and butter. ☐

We need eggs flour, sugar and butter. ☐

1 mark

24 Circle the word in the sentence that contains an **apostrophe** for **possession**.

Charlie didn't hide Sophie's glasses but he wasn't helping her look either.

1 mark

25 Explain why the underlined words start with a **capital letter**.

Shan spent the day at Kempshott Football Club with his dad and Tony.

_____

_____

1 mark

26 Tick the correct word to complete the sentence below.

We'll go to the beach next week _____ it rains tomorrow.

Tick **one**.

yet	☐
before	☐
if	☐
until	☐

1 mark

27 Tick **one** box in each row to show whether the **possessive apostrophe** has been used correctly or incorrectly.

Sentence	Correct	Incorrect
Ivan's hair was growing long.		
The horse's stable has a leak.		
Kerrys' story was about a bee.		

2 marks

28 The prefix re can be added to the root word play to make the word **replay**.
Tick the meaning of the word **replay**.

Tick **one**.

to play quickly ☐

to play unfairly ☐

to play again ☐

to play tomorrow ☐

1 mark

Total: _____ /30

Year 3: Spring Half Term Test 2

| Name: | Year: | Date: |

Spring Half Term 2

1 Write **one** word on the line below to complete the sentence in the **past tense**.

We _____ to the wildlife park at the weekend.

1 mark

2 Tick the correct word to complete the sentence below.

We were _____ the penguins swim.

Tick **one**.

watched ☐

watches ☐

watching ☐

watch ☐

1 mark

3 Which punctuation mark should be used in the space indicated by the arrow?

I rode my bike to Kim's house ↑ It was a hot day.

Tick **one**.

comma ☐

question mark ☐

apostrophe ☐

full stop ☐

1 mark

4 Draw a line to match each group of words to its contraction.

you have		it's
did not		I'll
I will		didn't
it is		you've

1 mark

5 Which one **prefix** can be added to all three words below to make new words?
Write the prefix in the box.

_____market

_____star

_____glue

[   ]

1 mark

6 Circle the **adverb** in the sentence below.

I   politely   opened   the   door   for   the   visitor.

1 mark

7 Which is the correct verb form to complete the sentence below?

After Sam _____ her coat, she met her mum at the gate.

Tick **one**.

is collecting ☐

has collected ☐

had collected ☐

was collecting ☐

1 mark

8 Add **inverted commas** to the sentence below to show what Harry is saying.

Have you seen my blue jumper, Mum? asked Harry.

1 mark

9 Insert the missing punctuation mark to complete the sentence below.

What a great job you have done tidying your room

1 mark

10 Explain why the underlined words start with a **capital letter**.

Ruby went to the Natural History Museum in London.

_____

_____

1 mark

11 Which option uses **verbs** correctly?

Tick **one**.

Raj saw his friend at the shop and wave. ☐

Raj saw his friend at the shop and waved. ☐

Raj sees his friend at the shop and wave. ☐

Raj sees his friend at the shop and waved. ☐

1 mark

12 Write the words <u>do not</u> as one word, using an **apostrophe**.

We _____ go to school on Saturdays.

1 mark

13 Which **word class** is the underlined word in the sentence below?

There was a knock on the door and Dad <u>immediately</u> jumped up to open it.

Tick **one**.

conjunction ☐

adverb ☐

verb ☐

determiner ☐

1 mark

14 Which option completes the sentence in the **present perfect**?

Jamil _____ his homework.

Tick **one**.

was finishing ☐

has finished ☐

finished ☐

had finished ☐

1 mark

15 Write a **command** a teacher might say at the end of the school day.
Remember to use correct punctuation.

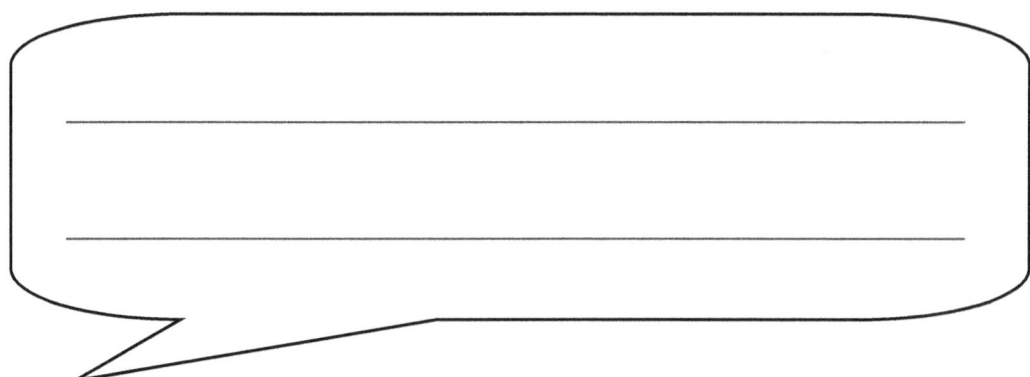

2 marks

16 Complete the sentences, using the **simple past** tense of the verbs in the boxes.

This morning I _____ with trains with my baby brother.

play

Then I _____ my ball around the garden.

kick

After that I _____ a cake with my big sister.

bake

1 mark

17 Replace the underlined words in the sentences below with their expanded forms.

We're going to the park soon, so I'll ride my bike then.

[ ]   [ ]

We won't have dinner until later this evening.

[ ]

1 mark

18 Draw a line to match each **prefix** to a word to make **four** different words.
Use each prefix only once.

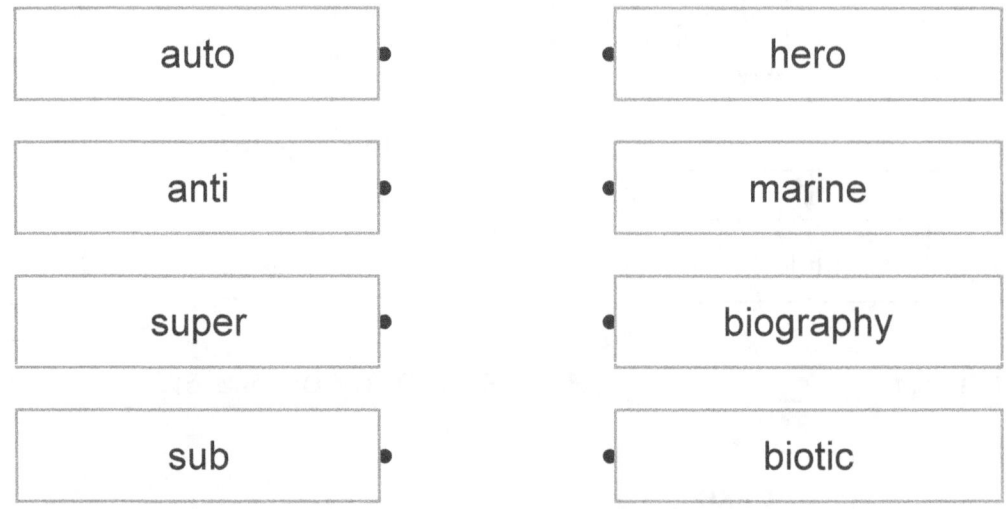

1 mark

19 Write the name of the punctuation mark used at the end of the sentence below.

How wonderful it is to see you again!

_____

1 mark

20 Circle the **adverb** in the sentence below.

My cousins live nearby.

1 mark

21 Which sentence uses **inverted commas** correctly?

Tick **one**.

Sunny said, Let's play in the woods today." ☐

Sunny said, "Let's play" in the woods today. ☐

Sunny said, "Let's play in the woods today." ☐

"Sunny said, Let's play in the woods today." ☐

1 mark

22 Tick **one** box in each row to show whether each sentence is written in the **present perfect** or the **simple past**.

Sentence	Present perfect	Simple past
Tom went out to play.		
Fatima has gone to the cinema.		
Olive has left her coat behind.		

2 marks

23 The sentence below should be in the **past progressive** tense. Circle **one** word that needs to be changed.

Elliot is thinking about a name for his new pet fish.

1 mark

24 Complete the sentence with an appropriate **adverb**.

Yasha folded her clothes _____.

1 mark

25 Circle the word in the passage that contains an **apostrophe** for **omission**.

Alex's mum said we can go swimming. Let's ask if Patrick can come too?

1 mark

26 Tick **two** boxes to show the correct places for **inverted commas** in the sentence below.

Tick **two**.

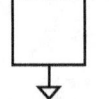 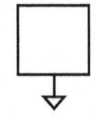 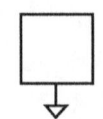 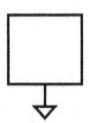

We are going to be late so hurry up! said Angela.

1 mark

Tick **one** box in each row to show whether the underlined word in each sentence is an **adverb of time** or an **adverb of place**.

Sentence	Adverb of time	Adverb of place
She lives over <u>there</u>.		
My pencil isn't <u>here</u>.		
We <u>recently</u> went shopping.		

2 marks

Total: _____ /30

Year 3: Summer Half Term Test 1

| Name: | Year: | Date: |

Summer Half Term 1

1 Tick the correct word to complete the sentence below.

We were _____ to our favourite song.

Tick **one**.

- listened ☐
- listens ☐
- listening ☐
- listen ☐

1 mark

2 Add **two** full stops in the correct places below.

The plane finally emerged from the clouds I could see the fields below

1 mark

3 Tick the correct option to complete the sentence below.

Dad bought Sasha ____ new puzzle.

Tick **one**.

- some ☐
- an ☐
- a ☐
- those ☐

1 mark

4 Write the correct word on the line in the sentence below.

tempted   attempts   temptation

It took Helen many _____ to complete the puzzle.

1 mark

5 Tick the correct word to complete the sentence below.

Drew loved sitting in the armchair _____ it was so comfortable.

Tick **one**.

therefore ☐

because ☐

consequently ☐

thus ☐

1 mark

6 Which option completes the sentence in the **present perfect**?

Tina _____ her money already.

Tick **one**.

is spending ☐

has spent ☐

had spent ☐

was spending ☐

1 mark

7 Tick **one** box in each row to show whether each sentence is in the **past progressive** or **present progressive**.

Sentence	Past progressive	Present progressive
The fish is swimming in circles.		
The bird was singing a sweet tune.		
The cow was resting under a tree.		

2 marks

8 Insert the missing punctuation mark to complete the sentence below.

What would you like to eat

1 mark

9 What does the root word <u>cent</u> mean in the word family below?

century   **cent**ipede   per**cent**   **cent**imetre

Tick **one**.

one ☐

ten ☐

one hundred ☐

one thousand ☐

1 mark

10 The sentence below should be in the **present progressive** tense. Circle **one** word that needs to be changed.

The explorer was searching for the opening to a deep cave.

1 mark

11 Draw a line to match each sentence to the correct **determiner**. Use each determiner only once.

Sentence	Determiner
Jake gave me _____ ball.	an
It is _____ best ball in the world.	the
I've had _____ amazing day.	a

1 mark

12 Which **word class** is the underlined word in the sentence below?

The supermarket is open <u>from</u> 7 a.m. till 11 p.m.

Tick **one**.

- determiner ☐
- adverb ☐
- preposition ☐
- verb ☐

1 mark

13 Explain why the underlined words start with **a capital letter**.

Gavin Brown is joining Stripes Primary Academy this September.

_____

_____

1 mark

14 Complete each of the sentences below with a word formed from the root word cover.

The pirate _____ a chest of treasure.

Mum _____ the plate of food to keep it warm.

1 mark

15 Which option completes the sentence in the **present perfect**?

Annie _____ in muddy puddles.

Tick **one**.

was splashing	☐
has splashed	☐
is splashing	☐
had splashed	☐

1 mark

16 Choose the correct word to complete each sentence. Write the word on the line.

I watched _____ television programme about a sea turtle.
　　　　　　　↓
　　　　　[a / an]

It swam across _____ ocean.
　　　　　　　↓
　　　　　[a / an]

The sea turtle's journey took _____ long time.
　　　　　　　↓
　　　　　[a / an]

1 mark

17 Circle the **preposition** in the sentence below.

The cat hid under the stairs.

1 mark

18 Tick **one** box in each row to show whether each sentence is written in the **present perfect** or the **simple past**.

Sentence	Present perfect	Simple past
Clare has eaten her biscuit.		
The dinosaur stomped through the forest.		
Ethan has won a competition.		

2 marks

19 Write a **statement** about your favourite meal. Remember to use correct punctuation.

_____

_____

2 marks

20 Which option completes the sentence in the **present perfect**?

I had a hole in my sock, but Dad _____ it up now.

Tick **one**.

had sewn	☐
has sewn	☐
sews	☐
was sewing	☐

1 mark

21 Which **word class** are the underlined words in the sentence below?

We discovered a secret door in an old garden wall.

Tick **one**.

conjunctions	☐
adverbs	☐
verbs	☐
determiners	☐

1 mark

22 What does the root word <u>graph</u> mean in the word family below?

autograph   graphic   photograph   telegraph

Tick **one**.

light ☐
listen ☐
write ☐
move ☐

1 mark

23 The verb in the sentence below should be in the **present progressive**. Circle **one** word that needs to be changed.

Verity was drawing a picture of her grandmother's house.

1 mark

24 Tick the **preposition** in the sentence below.

Tick **one**.

The hens are happily roosting in the hen house.
    ☐   ☐   ☐   ☐

1 mark

25 Which punctuation mark should be used in the space indicated by the arrow?

Jake opened Olive↑s blue lunchbox.

Tick **one**.

- question mark ☐
- full stop ☐
- apostrophe ☐
- comma ☐

1 mark

26 Write the correct word on the line in the sentence below.

informed   misinform   information

The detective needed all of the _____ before he could begin his investigation.

1 mark

27 Tick the sentence that is correct.

Tick **one**.

- Priti is wearing an new jumper. ☐
- Priti is wearing some new jumper. ☐
- Priti is wearing these new jumper. ☐
- Priti is wearing a new jumper. ☐

1 mark

Total: _____ /30

Summer Half Term 2

1 Add a **suffix** to the words in the boxes to complete the sentences.

Trying to play cricket in a storm was _____.

point

We were _____ when we walked past the glass shelves.

care

1 mark

2 Write the correct word on the line in the sentence below.

small   smaller   smallest

The children compared shoe sizes. Mark's were smaller than Tom's, but Yasmin's were the _____.

1 mark

3 Tick the **adverb** in the sentence below.

Tick **one**.

The large green toad hopped lazily around the garden pond.

1 mark

Year 3: Summer Half Term Test 2

4 Underline the **noun phrase** in the sentence below.

Princess Alice combed her long golden hair.

1 mark

5 Which option is a **noun phrase**?

Tick **one**.

quite rudely ☐

as quick as a flash ☐

had been shouting ☐

the first train stop ☐

1 mark

6 Tick **one** box in each row to show whether the sentence is a **command** or a **statement**.

Sentence	Command	Statement
Put that stapler back.		
You didn't ask to borrow it.		
Ask for permission next time.		

2 marks

7 Which sentence contains a verb in the **past progressive**?

Tick **one**.

Sarah is chatting on the phone. ☐

Sarah was chatting on the phone. ☐

Sarah chatted on the phone. ☐

Sarah will chat on the phone. ☐

1 mark

8 Which **tense** is used in the sentence below?

I'm sure my gerbil was planning her escape route.

Tick **one**.

simple past ☐

simple present ☐

past progressive ☐

present progressive ☐

1 mark

9 Which sentence uses **capital letters** correctly?

Tick **one**.

In August, steven is going to Spain. ☐

In August, Steven is going to Spain. ☐

In August, Steven is going to spain. ☐

In august, Steven is going to Spain. ☐

1 mark

10 Tick **one** box to show where a **comma** should go in the sentence below.

Tick **one**.

I go swimming every Monday Tuesday and Friday.

☐   ☐   ☐   ☐

1 mark

11 Insert an **apostrophe** in the correct place in the sentence below.

Mr Patels car is sparkling clean.

1 mark

12 Draw a line to match each group of words to its contraction.

can not	hasn't
has not	won't
they have	can't
will not	they've

1 mark

13 Which one **prefix** can be added to all three words below to make new words?
Write the prefix in the box.

_____heading

_____marine

_____contractor

1 mark

14 Choose the correct word to complete each sentence.
Write the word on the line.

I heard _____ owl screeching outside.

[a / an]

I went out and saw it was _____ barn owl.

[a / an]

It flew along the hedgerow and behind _____ tree.

[a / an]

1 mark

15 What does the root word <u>oct</u> mean in the word family below?

October   **oct**opus   **oct**agon   **oct**agonal

Tick **one**.

month ☐

shape ☐

legs ☐

eight ☐

1 mark

16 Tick the correct word to complete the sentence below.

Mum goes to work at night _____ we all sleep.

Tick **one**.

- therefore ☐
- before ☐
- so ☐
- while ☐

1 mark

17 Complete the sentence with an appropriate **adverb**.

The monkey swung _____ through the trees.

1 mark

18 Which **word class** is the underlined word in the sentence below?

The old dog slept <u>beside</u> the fireplace.

Tick **one**.

- determiner ☐
- preposition ☐
- noun ☐
- verb ☐

1 mark

19 Which option completes the sentence in the **present perfect**?

Rumi _____ around the entire town.

Tick **one**.

was walking ☐

has walked ☐

walks ☐

had walked ☐

1 mark

20 Add **inverted commas** to the sentence below to show what Ravi is saying.

Ravi declared, I would like to be a fire-fighter.

1 mark

21 Which sentence must end with a **question mark**?

Tick **one**.

They wondered when he would arrive ☐

What would you like to eat ☐

What a great plan we have thought of ☐

I'm excited and I can't wait to leave ☐

1 mark

22 Which option is punctuated correctly?

Tick **one**.

The lion yawned. It lay down and shut its eyes. ☐

The lion yawned it lay down and shut its eyes. ☐

the lion yawned. it lay down and shut its eyes. ☐

The lion yawned. It lay down and shut its eyes ☐

1 mark

23 Add **two commas** to the sentence below to make it clear that Kim has four things on her plate.

Kim has a sandwich an apple some cucumber and a pile of crisps on her plate.

1 mark

24 Tick **one** box in each row to show whether the **possessive apostrophe** has been used correctly or incorrectly.

Sentence	Correct	Incorrect
Petra's cute kittens are resting.		
We borrowed Danny's pens.		
Jessicas room is a mess'.		

2 marks

25 Replace the underlined words in the sentences below with their expanded forms.

Let's go outside and play catch, it's such a fun game.

[ ]   [ ]

It doesn't matter that there are only two of us.

[ ]

1 mark

26 Complete the sentence with an appropriate **adverb**.

She walked down the path _____.

1 mark

27 Tick the correct word to complete the sentence below.

I brush my teeth every night _____ I go to bed.

Tick **one**.

before   ☐

after   ☐

because   ☐

so   ☐

1 mark

28 What is the grammatical term for the underlined part of the sentence?

<u>My rainbow-coloured leather suitcase</u> was in the car.

Tick **one**.

exclamation ☐

main clause ☐

noun phrase ☐

command ☐

1 mark

Total: _____ /30

Mark scheme for Autumn Half Term 1

Qu.	Requirement	Mark
1 G1 G6	**Award 1 mark** for all four lines drawn correctly: *spiteful, pointless, delightful, endless*	1m
2 G5	**Award 1 mark** for a comma placed after the word *apple*.	1m
3 G4	**Award 1 mark** for the word *wear* circled.	1m
4 G2	**Award 1 mark** for a tick next to the second sentence: Where did you put your bag?	1m
5 G6	**Award 1 mark** for the words *cheerful* and *sleepless* written on the lines.	1m
6 G3	**Award 1 mark** for the noun phrase *the big red bus* underlined.	1m
7 G5	**Award 1 mark** for a tick next to the first option: don't	1m
8 G5	**Award 2 marks** for all three boxes ticked correctly: When can we go to the library = Question mark When the music plays, I will sing = Full stop When will the film start = Question mark **Additional guidance** • Award 1 mark if two boxes are ticked correctly.	2m
9 G5	**Award 1 mark** for the word *hasn't* written in the box.	1m
10 G2	**Award 2 marks** for all three boxes ticked correctly: The leaves are turning yellow = Statement I think I will need gloves today = Statement What a cold morning it is = Exclamation **Additional guidance** • Award 1 mark if two boxes are ticked correctly.	2m
11 G4	**Award 1 mark** for a tick next to the third sentence: The cat is eating her dinner.	1m
12 G2	**Award 2 marks** for an appropriate, grammatically correct command using an imperative verb in a main clause with correct punctuation. **Award 1 mark** for an appropriate, grammatically correct command using an imperative verb in a main clause with incorrect punctuation. **Additional guidance** • Correct punctuation refers to the correct use of capital letters, full stops and/or exclamation marks – other incorrect or omitted punctuation should not be penalised. • Incorrect spelling should not be penalised. • Markers are encouraged to credit imaginative interpretations of the context.	2m
13 G5	**Award 1 mark** for commas placed after the words *lamp* and *book*.	1m

Year 3: Autumn Half Term Test 1 – Mark scheme

Qu.	Requirement	Mark
14 G4	**Award 1 mark** for the word *is* circled.	1m
15 G5	**Award 1 mark** for a tick next to the third option: Ann loves writing stories. She writes every day.	1m
16 G5	**Award 1 mark** for the words *my* and *tuesday* circled.	1m
17 G3	**Award 1 mark** for a tick next to the second option: noun phrase	1m
18 G4	**Award 2 marks** for all three boxes ticked correctly: Kate was tidying up. = Past progressive Joshi is listening to music. = Present progressive Bill is walking his dog. = Present progressive **Additional guidance** • Award 1 mark if two boxes are ticked correctly.	2m
19 G5	**Award 1 mark** for an apostrophe after the letter *r* in *Peters*: Those are Peter's pencils.	1m
20 G1	**Award 1 mark** for a tick next to the second option: an	1m
21 G4	**Award 1 mark** for a tick next to the fourth option: was painting	1m
22 G1	**Award 1 mark** for a tick next to the third option: before	1m
23 G5	**Award 1 mark** for correct placement of inverted commas: "Can we go for a bike ride?" asked Imran.	1m
24 G3	**Award 1 mark** for a tick next to the third option: a noun phrase	1m
25 G4	**Award 1 mark** for the word *was* circled.	1m
26 G1	**Award 1 mark** for *a* (a frog), *an* (an envelope) and *an* (an hour) written on the lines.	1m

Mark scheme for Autumn Half Term 2

Qu.	Requirement	Mark
1 G1 G6	**Award 1 mark** for the word *taller* written on the line.	1m
2 G4	**Award 1 mark** for a tick next to the second option: Zack was playing cricket.	1m
3 G5	**Award 1 mark** for a question mark added to the end of the sentence: Can you count to one hundred?	1m
4 G1	**Award 1 mark** for all three lines drawn correctly: At the beach I ate <u>an</u> ice-cream. I saw <u>a</u> big seagull. I thought it was <u>the</u> best day ever.	1m
5 G5	**Award 1 mark** for correct placement of inverted commas: "I would like pizza for dinner tonight," said Lara.	1m
6 G1	**Award 1 mark** for a tick next to the second option: adverb	1m
7 G6	**Award 1 mark** for adding the suffix *er* to make the word *faster*.	1m
8 G5	**Award 1 mark** for an explanation that refers to capital letters being required for people, places and days of the week.	1m
9 G1	**Award 1 mark** for a tick next to the fourth option: an	1m
10 G5	**Award 1 mark** for a tick next to the third option: "Would you like to play?" asked Robert.	1m
11 G5	**Award 1 mark** for a tick next to the second option: exclamation mark	1m
12 G1 G6	**Award 1 mark** for the word *tastier* written on the line.	1m
13 G4	**Award 1 mark** for the word *is* circled.	1m
14 G1	**Award 1 mark** for all three lines drawn correctly: I made <u>a</u> model robot. I used <u>an</u> old plastic bottle. Then added bits of wood for <u>the</u> feet.	1m
15 G2	**Award 1 mark** for a tick next to the fourth option: What a great story you've written!	1m
16 G6	**Award 1 mark** for adding the suffix *er* to make the word *cheaper*.	1m

Year 3: Autumn Half Term Test 2 – Mark scheme

Qu.	Requirement	Mark
17 G1	**Award 2 marks** for all three boxes ticked correctly: I will speak to you soon. = Adverb of time I saw that show yesterday. = Adverb of time I played the game outdoors. = Adverb of place **Additional guidance** • Award 1 mark if two boxes are ticked correctly.	2m
18 G2	**Award 2 marks** for an appropriate, grammatically correct statement with correct punctuation. **Award 1 mark** for an appropriate, grammatically correct statement with incorrect punctuation. **Additional guidance** • Correct punctuation refers to the correct use of capital letters, full stops and/or exclamation marks – other incorrect or omitted punctuation should not be penalised. • Incorrect spelling should not be penalised. Markers are encouraged to credit imaginative interpretations of the context.	2m
19 G4	**Award 2 marks** for all three boxes ticked correctly: Emma was playing chess. = Past progressive Stan is jumping on the trampoline. = Present progressive Pia was brushing her hair. = Past progressive **Additional guidance** • Award 1 mark if two boxes are ticked correctly.	2m
20 G1	**Award 1 mark** for *a* (a film), *an* (an ant) and *a* (a big glass) written on the lines.	1m
21 G1 G6	**Award 1 mark** for the word *happiest* written on the line.	1m
22 G1	**Award 1 mark** for a tick next to the fourth option: adverb	1m
23 G5	**Award 1 mark** for correct placement of inverted commas: Oscar shouted, "Stop kicking my ball over the fence!"	1m
24 G1	**Award 1 mark** for a tick next to the third option: determiners	1m
25 G4	**Award 1 mark** for a tick next to the third option: past progressive	1m
26 G5	**Award 1 mark** for ticks in the second and fourth boxes.	1m
27 G1	**Award 1 mark** for a tick in the fourth box: indoors	1m

Mark scheme for Spring Half Term 1

Qu.	Requirement	Mark
1 G1 G6	**Award 1 mark** for the word *carefully* circled.	1m
2 G4	**Award 1 mark** for the word *was* circled.	1m
3 G5	**Award 1 mark** for a tick next to the fourth option: Jed Jones, the pop star, is visiting Hull today.	1m
4 G5	**Award 1 mark** for a tick in the second box.	1m
5 G5	**Award 1 mark** for an apostrophe after the second letter *e* in *Isabelles*: That is Isabelle's skipping rope.	1m
6 G1 G6	**Award 1 mark** for all four lines drawn correctly: *supermarket, antibody, autograph, interview*	1m
7 G1 G6	**Award 1 mark** for the word *solution* written on the line.	1m
8 G1	**Award 1 mark** for a tick next to the second option: before	1m
9 G1	**Award 1 mark** for a tick in the third box: loudly	1m
10 G5	**Award 1 mark** for an exclamation mark added to the end of the sentence: What a fast racing car that is!	1m
11 G5	**Award 1 mark** for a tick next to the first option: Jess went to Todd's party at the weekend.	1m
12 G4	**Award 2 marks** for all three boxes ticked correctly: Maya was riding her bike. = Past progressive Eden is playing the trumpet. = Present progressive Adam is eating his dinner. = Present progressive **Additional guidance** • Award 1 mark if two boxes are ticked correctly.	2m
13 G6	**Award 1 mark** for a tick next to the second option: sound	1m
14 G5	**Award 1 mark** for commas placed after the words *purse* and *hairbrush*.	1m
15 G1 G6	**Award 1 mark** for the prefix *sub* written in the box.	1m
16 G5	**Award 1 mark** for a tick next to the third option: apostrophe	1m
17 G6	**Award 1 mark** for any appropriate word formed from the root *thought*, for example: *thoughtful, thoughtless*.	1m
18 G1	**Award 1 mark** for any appropriate adverb, for example: *carefully, gently, softly, timidly*.	1m

Year 3: Spring Half Term Test 1 – Mark scheme

Qu.	Requirement	Mark
19 G4	**Award 1 mark** for a tick next to the third option: is mowing	1m
20 G5	**Award 1 mark** for a tick next to the fourth option: Janice works in a shop. Her shift starts at ten.	1m
21 G1 G6	**Award 1 mark** for all four lines drawn correctly: *submarine, reaction, transformation, mistake*	1m
22 G1	**Award 1 mark** for the word *yet* circled.	1m
23 G5	**Award 1 mark** for a tick next to the second option: We need eggs, flour, sugar and butter.	1m
24 G5	**Award 1 mark** for the word *Sophie's* circled.	1m
25 G5	**Award 1 mark** for an explanation that refers to capital letters being required for people and places.	1m
26 G1	**Award 1 mark** for a tick next to the third option: if	1m
27 G5	**Award 2 marks** for all three boxes ticked correctly: Ivan's hair was growing long. = Correct The horse's stable has a leak. = Correct Kerrys' story was about a bee. = Incorrect **Additional guidance** • Award 1 mark if two boxes are ticked correctly.	2m
28 G6	**Award 1 mark** for a tick next to the third option: to play again	1m

Mark scheme for Spring Half Term 2

Qu.	Requirement	Mark
1 G4	**Award 1 mark** for the use of any appropriate past tense verb, for example: *walked, went, popped, drove*.	1m
2 G4	**Award 1 mark** for a tick next to the third option: watching	1m
3 G5	**Award 1 mark** for a tick next to the fourth option: full stop	1m
4 G5	**Award 1 mark** for all four lines drawn correctly: you have = you've did not = didn't I will = I'll it is = it's	1m
5 G1 G6	**Award 1 mark** for the prefix *super* written in the box.	1m
6 G1	**Award 1 mark** for the word *politely* circled.	1m
7 G4	**Award 1 mark** for a tick next to the third option: had collected	1m
8 G5	**Award 1 mark** for correct placement of inverted commas: "Have you seen my blue jumper, Mum?" asked Harry.	1m
9 G5	**Award 1 mark** for an exclamation mark added to the end of the sentence: What a great job you have done tidying your room!	1m
10 G2	**Award 1 mark** for an explanation that refers to capital letters being required for people and places.	1m
11 G4	**Award 1 mark** for a tick next to the second option: Raj saw his friend at the shop and waved.	1m
12 G5	**Award 1 mark** for the word *don't* written on the line.	1m
13 G1	**Award 1 mark** for a tick next to the second option: adverb	1m
14 G4	**Award 1 mark** for a tick next to the second option: has finished	1m
15 G2	**Award 2 marks** for an appropriate, grammatically correct command using an imperative verb in a main clause with correct punctuation. **Award 1 mark** for an appropriate, grammatically correct command using an imperative verb in a main clause with incorrect punctuation. **Additional guidance** • Correct punctuation refers to the correct use of capital letters, full stops and/or exclamation marks – other incorrect or omitted punctuation should not be penalised. • Incorrect spelling should not be penalised. Markers are encouraged to credit imaginative interpretations of the context.	2m
16 G4	**Award 1 mark** for the words *played*, *kicked* and *baked* written on the lines.	1m

Year 3: Spring Half Term Test 2 – Mark scheme

Qu.	Requirement	Mark
17 G5	**Award 1 mark** for the words *We are*, *I will* and *will not* written on the lines.	1m
18 G1 G6	**Award 1 mark** for all four lines drawn correctly. *autobiography, antibiotic, superhero, submarine*	1m
19 G5	**Award 1 mark** for the words *exclamation mark* written on the line.	1m
20 G1	**Award 1 mark** for the word *nearby* circled.	1m
21 G5	**Award 1 mark** for a tick next to the third option: Sunny said, "Let's play in the woods today."	1m
22 G4	**Award 2 marks** for all three boxes ticked correctly: Tom went out to play. = Simple past Fatima has gone to the cinema. = Present perfect Olive has left her coat behind. = Present perfect **Additional guidance** • Award 1 mark if two boxes are ticked correctly.	2m
23 G4	**Award 1 mark** for the word *is* circled.	1m
24 G1	**Award 1 mark** for any appropriate adverb, for example: *carefully, neatly, quickly, slowly*.	1m
25 G5	**Award 1 mark** for the word *Let's* circled	1m
26 G5	**Award 1 mark** for ticks in the first and fourth boxes.	1m
27 G1	**Award 2 marks** for all three boxes ticked correctly: She lives over there. = Adverb of place My pencil isn't here. = Adverb of place We recently went shopping. = Adverb of time **Additional guidance** • Award 1 mark if two boxes are ticked correctly.	2m

Mark scheme for Summer Half Term 1

Qu.	Requirement	Mark
1 G4	**Award 1 mark** for a tick next to the third option: listening	1m
2 G5	**Award 1 mark** for full stops after the words *clouds* and *below*.	1m
3 G1	**Award 1 mark** for a tick next to the third option: a	1m
4 G1 G6	**Award 1 mark** for the word *attempts* written on the line.	1m
5 G1	**Award 1 mark** for a tick next to the second option: because	1m
6 G4	**Award 1 mark** for a tick next to the third option: has spent	1m
7 G4	**Award 2 marks** for all three boxes ticked correctly: The fish is swimming in circles. = Present progressive The bird was singing a sweet tune. = Past progressive The cow was resting under a tree. = Past progressive **Additional guidance** • Award 1 mark if two boxes are ticked correctly.	2m
8 G5	**Award 1 mark** for a question mark added at the end of the sentence.	1m
9 G6	**Award 1 mark** for a tick next to the third option: one hundred	1m
10 G4	**Award 1 mark** for the word *was* circled.	1m
11 G1	**Award 1 mark** for all three lines drawn correctly: Jake gave me a ball. It is the best ball in the world. I've had an amazing day.	1m
12 G1	**Award 1 mark** for a tick next to the third option: preposition	1m
13 G5	**Award 1 mark** for an explanation that refers to capital letters being required for people, places and months of the year.	1m
14 G6	**Award 1 mark** for any appropriate words formed from the root word *cover*, for example: *discovered, covered, recovered, uncovered*.	1m
15 G4	**Award 1 mark** for a tick next to the second option: has splashed	1m
16 G1	**Award 1 mark** for *a* (a television programme), *an* (an ocean) and *a* (a long time) written on the lines.	1m
17 G1	**Award 1 mark** for the word *under* circled.	1m

Year 3: Summer Half Term Test 1 – Mark scheme

Qu.	Requirement	Mark
18 G4	**Award 2 marks** for all three boxes ticked correctly: Clare has eaten her biscuit. = Present perfect The dinosaur stomped through the forest. = Simple past Ethan has won a competition. = Present perfect **Additional guidance** • Award 1 mark if two boxes are ticked correctly.	2m
19 G2 G5	**Award 2 marks** for an appropriate, grammatically correct statement with correct punctuation. **Award 1 mark** for an appropriate, grammatically correct statement with incorrect punctuation. **Additional guidance** • Correct punctuation refers to the correct use of capital letters, full stops and/or exclamation marks – other incorrect or omitted punctuation should not be penalised. • Incorrect spelling should not be penalised. Markers are encouraged to credit imaginative interpretations of the context.	2m
20 G4	**Award 1 mark** for a tick next to the second option: has sewn	1m
21 G1	**Award 1 mark** for a tick next to the fourth option: determiners	1m
22 G6	**Award 1 mark** for a tick next to the third option: write	1m
23 G4	**Award 1 mark** for the word *was* circled.	1m
24 G1	**Award 1 mark** for a tick in the third box: in	1m
25 G5	**Award 1 mark** for a tick next to the third option: apostrophe	1m
26 G1 G6	**Award 1 mark** for the word *information* written on the line.	1m
27 G1	**Award 1 mark** for a tick next to the fourth option: Priti is wearing a new jumper.	1m

Mark scheme for Summer Half Term 2

Qu.	Requirement	Mark
1 G6	**Award 1 mark** for the words *pointless* and *careful* written on the lines.	1m
2 G1 G6	**Award 1 mark** for the word *smallest* written on the line.	1m
3 G1 G6	**Award 1 mark** for a tick in the third box: *lazily*	1m
4 G3	**Award 1 mark** for the noun phrase *her long golden hair* underlined.	1m
5 G3	**Award 1 mark** for a tick next to the fourth option: *the first train stop*	1m
6 G2	**Award 2 marks** for all three boxes ticked correctly: Put that stapler back. = Command You didn't ask to borrow it. = Statement Ask for permission next time. = Command **Additional guidance** • Award 1 mark if two boxes are ticked correctly.	2m
7 G4	**Award 1 mark** for a tick next to the second option: *Sarah was chatting on the phone.*	1m
8 G4	**Award 1 mark** for a tick next to the third option: *past progressive*	1m
9 G5	**Award 1 mark** for a tick next to the second option: *In August, Steven is going to Spain.*	1m
10 G5	**Award 1 mark** for a tick in the third box.	1m
11 G5	**Award 1 mark** for an apostrophe after the letter *l* in *Patels*: Mr Patel's car is sparkling clean.	1m
12 G5	**Award 1 mark** for all four lines drawn correctly: can not – can't has not = hasn't they have = they've will not = won't	1m
13 G1 G6	**Award 1 mark** for the prefix *sub* written in the box.	1m
14 G1	**Award 1 mark** for *an* (an owl), *a* (a barn owl) and *a* (a tree) written on the lines.	1m
15 G6	**Award 1 mark** for a tick next to the fourth option: *eight*	1m
16 G1	**Award 1 mark** for a tick next to the fourth option: *while*	1m
17 G1	**Award 1 mark** for the use of any appropriate adverb, for example: *carefully, energetically, quickly, noisily.*	1m

Year 3: Summer Half Term Test 2 – Mark scheme

Qu.	Requirement	Mark
18 G1	**Award 1 mark** for a tick next to the second option: preposition	1m
19 G4	**Award 1 mark** for a tick next to the second option: has walked	1m
20 G5	**Award 1 mark** for the correct placement of inverted commas: Ravi declared, "I would like to be a fire-fighter."	1m
21 G5	**Award 1 mark** for a tick next to the second option: What would you like to eat	1m
22 G5	**Award 1 mark** for a tick next to the first option: The lion yawned. It lay down and shut its eyes.	1m
23 G5	**Award 1 mark** for commas placed after the words *sandwich* and *apple*.	1m
24 G5	**Award 2 marks** for all three boxes ticked correctly: Petra's cute kittens are resting. = Correct We borrowed Danny's pens. = Correct Jessicas room is a mess'. = Incorrect **Additional guidance** • Award 1 mark if two boxes are ticked correctly.	2m
25 G5	**Award 1 mark** for the words *Let us*, *it is* and *does not* written in the boxes.	1m
26 G1	**Award 1 mark** for the use of any appropriate adverb, for example: *slowly, quickly, noisily, quietly*.	1m
27 G1	**Award 1 mark** for a tick next to the first option: before	1m
28 G3	**Award 1 mark** for a tick next to the third option: noun phrase	1m

Name: Class:

Year 3 Grammar, Punctuation and Vocabulary Record Sheet

Tests	Mark	Total marks	Key skills to target
Autumn Half Term Test 1			
Autumn Half Term Test 2			
Spring Half Term Test 1			
Spring Half Term Test 2			
Summer Half Term Test 1			
Summer Half Term Test 2